Many Kinds of Matter

A Look at Solids, Liquids, and Gases

Jennifer Boothroyd

Lerner Publications
Minneapolis

For my hubby,
who keeps me
on solid ground

Lerner Publications Company
A division of Lerner Publishing Group, Inc.
241 First Avenue North
Minneapolis, MN 55401 USA

For reading levels and more information, look up this title at www.lernerbooks.com.

Library of Congress Cataloging-in-Publication Data

Boothroyd, Jennifer, 1972–
    Many kinds of matter : a look at solids, liquids, and gases / by Jennifer Boothroyd.
       p.   cm. — (Lightning bolt books™— Exploring physical science)
    Includes index.
    ISBN 978–0–7613–6096–4 (lib. bdg. : alk. paper)
    ISBN 978–0–7613–7225–7 (EB pdf)
    1. Matter—Properties—Juvenile literature. 2. Change of state (Physics)—Juvenile literature.
    I. Title.
    QC173.36.B66 2011
    530.4—dc22   2010027980

Manufactured in the United States of America
4 — CG — 2/1/15

Contents

Matter

Matter is everywhere. Matter is anything that has mass and volume. Mass is the amount of material in an object. Volume is the amount of space an object takes up.

Trees, lakes, and people are matter. All have mass and volume.

There are three kinds of matter. The three kinds of matter are solids, liquids, and gases.

Solids

Books, rocks, and toys are solids.

Books are one example of a solid.

Solid matter holds its own shape. Solids do not take the shape of their container. Marbles fill a jar. But the marbles are still round.

The shape of solids does not change when you put them in a container.

WE
RECYCLE

Solids are not easy to compress. *Compress* means to squeeze something into a tight space. Bottles and cans are solids. It's not easy to squeeze them into this recycling bin!

Solids do not flow. Solid candies don't spread across ice cream the way hot fudge sauce does.

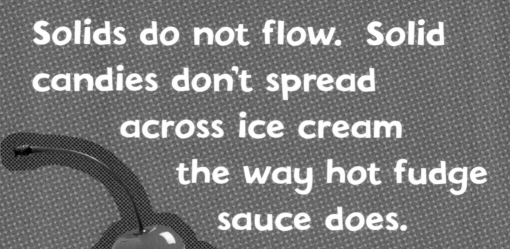

Candy sprinkles are solids. They do not flow over ice cream.

Liquids

Oil, syrup, and water are liquids.

Oil is one example of a liquid.

Liquid matter does not hold its own shape. Liquids take the shape of their container. Water inside a swimming pool takes on the shape of the pool.

Water in a square pool takes on a square shape.

Liquids are not easy to compress. Milk is a liquid.

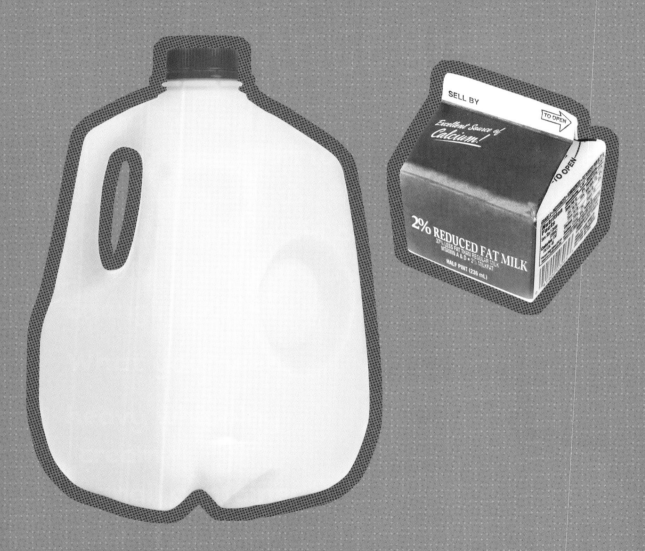

You couldn't fit the milk in the jug into the little carton.

Liquids flow. Liquid syrup spreads across pancakes.

Gases

Air, steam, and your breath are gases.

Your breath is one example of a gas.

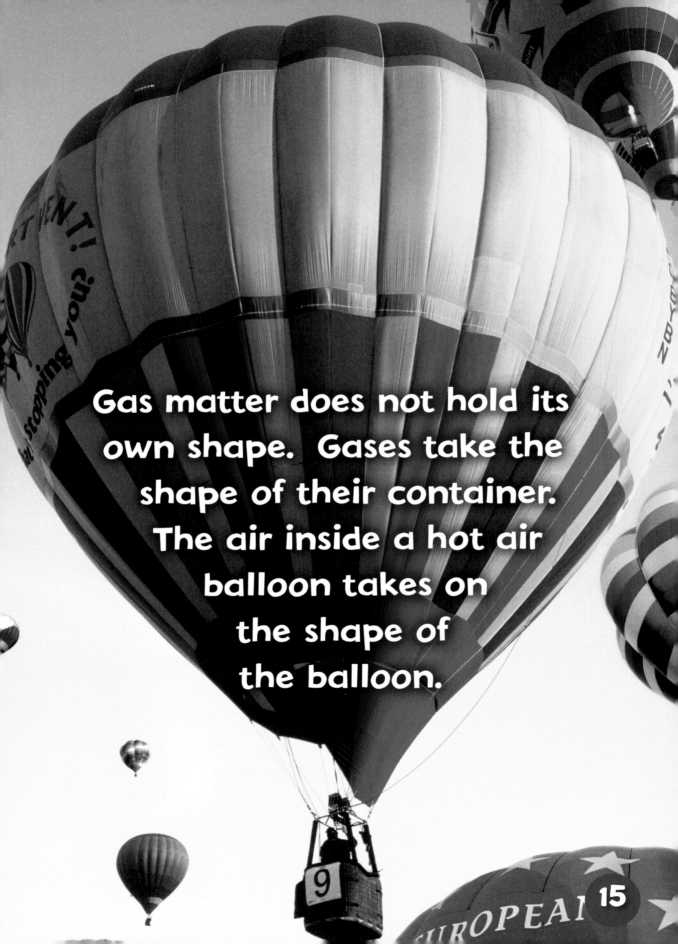

Gas matter does not hold its own shape. Gases take the shape of their container. The air inside a hot air balloon takes on the shape of the balloon.

Gases are easy to compress. Carbon dioxide is a gas. It's inside soda cans. It's squeezed into the cans to give the soda bubbles.

Carbon dioxide rushes out of soda cans when you open them.

Gases flow. The air inside a bubble spreads to fill the space inside the bubble.

Matter and Changes

Matter can change from one kind to another.

Some solids can change to liquids. Some liquids can change to gases.

The liquid in this cup is changing to a gas.

Water is a special kind of matter. You know that water is a liquid. But it can easily be found in all three forms on our planet.

Water becomes a solid if it is cooled. It turns into ice.

Water turns into ice when it freezes. Water freezes when it reaches a temperature of 32°F (0°C).

Water becomes a gas if it is heated. It turns into steam.

Water turns into steam when it boils. Water boils when it reaches a temperature of 212°F (100°C).

Water at any temperature can change into water vapor. Water vapor is a gas. This change is called evaporation.

Some people use a drying rack after washing their dishes. The dishes dry after the water evaporates.

Water vapor changes back into liquid water when it cools in the air. This change is called condensation. You can see condensation after a hot shower. The water vapor touches the shower door and turns back into a liquid.

Have you ever seen condensation on a shower door?

Other matter can change forms too. Cheese is a solid. It melts when it gets hot. It changes to a liquid.

Bread dipped in melted cheese is a tasty treat.

Juice is a liquid. It freezes
when it gets cold. It changes
to a solid.

Ice pops can be
made by freezing
juice.

Dry ice is a solid. Dry ice is frozen carbon dioxide. It changes back into a gas as it warms up.

Dry ice gives off mist as it changes to a gas. Many people use it in Halloween decorations. But it can be dangerous and must be used carefully.

We use solids, liquids, and gases every day. They are an important part of our lives and our planet.

Activity
Tasty Changing Matter

Lots of people love to eat butter. They spread it on toast, on potatoes, and on asparagus. But did you know that this tasty solid actually comes from a liquid? Try this activity to change liquid cream into solid butter.

What you need:

heavy whipping
  cream
a small container
  with a lid
a pinch of salt
  (optional)

What you do:

1. Take the whipping cream out of the refrigerator. Let it sit at room temperature for a few minutes.

2. Fill the container halfway with the whipping cream.

3. Tightly seal the container with the lid.

4. Shake the container back and forth. Keep shaking for about ten minutes, or until the cream sticks together in a clump.

5. Open the lid. There may be a bit of liquid left in the container. It's called buttermilk. Pour off the buttermilk.

6. Your butter is ready to enjoy! If you'd like, you can mix a pinch of salt in with your butter. Then give it a taste.

Glossary

compress: to squeeze something into a tight space

condensation: the change that happens when a gas becomes a liquid

evaporation: the change that happens when a liquid becomes a gas

gas: a substance that will spread to fill any space that contains it

liquid: a wet substance that you can pour

mass: the amount of material in an object

matter: anything that has mass and volume

solid: something that is often hard and firm and is neither a liquid nor a gas

volume: the amount of space an object takes up

water vapor: the gas produced when water evaporates

Further Reading

Bitesize Science: Changing State
http://www.bbc.co.uk/schools/ks2bitesize/science/
materials/changing_state/play.shtml

Boothroyd, Jennifer. *How Big? How Heavy? How Dense?: A Look at Matter.* **Minneapolis: Lerner Publications Company, 2011.**

FOSSWeb: Change It!
http://www.fossweb.com/modulesK-2/
SolidsandLiquids/activities/changeit.html

Garrett, Ginger. *Solids, Liquids, and Gases.* **New York: Children's Press, 2004.**

Spilsbury, Richard, and Louise Spilsbury. *What Are Solids, Liquids, and Gases?: Exploring Science with Hands-On Activities.* **Berkeley Heights, NJ: Enslow Elementary, 2008.**

Index

Photo Acknowledgments

The images in this book are used with the permission of: © Sunflowersister/
Dreamstime.com, p. 2; © rubberball/Getty Images, p. 4; © iStockphoto.com/williv, p. 5
(top left); © Stephen Smith/Photonica/Getty Images, p. 5 (top right); © Dmitry
Kudryavtsev/Dreamstime.com, p. 5 (bottom); © Les Palenik/Dreamstime.com, p. 6;
© Shaffer/Smith/SuperStock, p. 7; © Stockbyte, p. 8; © iStockphoto.com/DNY59, p. 9;
© Olga Lyubkin/Dreamstime.com, p. 10; © iStockphoto.com/frankoppermann, p. 11;
© Michael Flippo/Dreamstime.com, p. 12 (left); © Suzanne Tucker/Dreamstime.com,
p. 12 (right); © Charles Gullung/Taxi/Getty Images, p. 13; © Noam Armonn/Dreamstime.
com, p. 14; Brand X Pictures, p. 15; © Keith Bell/Dreamstime.com, p. 16; © Kablonk/
SuperStock, p. 17; © Photodisc/Getty Images, p. 18; © Achim Baqué/Dreamstime.com,
p. 19 (top); © Kenneth Keifer/Dreamstime.com, p. 19 (center); © Tamara Kulikova/
Dreamstime.com, p. 19 (bottom); © Na Gen Imaging/Workbook Stock/Getty Images,
p.20; © Trevor Chriss/Alamy, p. 21; © Tom Schierlitz/The Image Bank/Getty Images,
p. 22; © Ian Grant/Dreamstime.com, p. 23; © Jeannette Lambert/Dreamstime.com,
p. 24; © Foodcollection RF/Getty Images, p. 25; © Rami Aapasuo/Alamy, p. 26;
© Radius Images/Getty Images, p. 27; © Dorling Kindersley/Getty Images, p. 28 (top
left); © Vasiliy Vishnevskiy/Dreamstime.com, p. 28 (bottom left); © Eric Inghels/
Dreamstime.com, p. 28 (right); © Tatiana Sevryugina/Dreamstime.com, p. 30;
© Hongqi Zhang/Dreamstime.com, p. 31.

Front cover: © Vlue/Dreamstime.com (ice cube tray); © Can Balcioglu/Dreamstime.com
(kettle); © Elena Elisseeva/Dreamstime.com (faucet).